OWLS
Hunters of the Night

Margaret Wheeler Sadoway

Lerner Publications Company ■ Minneapolis

ACKNOWLEDGMENTS: All photographs in this book copyright © Tom Stack and Associates. Pp. 4, 18, Alan G. Nelson; pp. 7 (left), 32, 56, John Gerlach; pp. 7 (right), 38, Jan L. Wassink; pp. 10, 25, 52, Charles G. Summers, Jr.; pp. 14, 43, Leonard Lee Rue III; p. 16, Tom Brakefield; p. 21, Phil and Loretta Hermann; pp. 25, 58, Joe McDonald; pp. 1, 35, Charles Andre; p. 45, Raymond Coleman; p. 48, Tom J. Ulrich; p. 50, R. Gildart. Cover photograph by R. Gildart.

For Kate, Nancy, Aaron, Taya, and Chaz,
with the hope that all of these owls will still exist when they grow up

LIBRARY OF CONGRESS CATALOGING IN PUBLICATION DATA

Sadoway, Margaret Wheeler.
Owls: hunters of the night.

(Nature books for young readers)
Includes index.
SUMMARY: Text and photographs describe the physical characteristics, habits, and behavior of 18 species of owls that make their homes in North America.

1. Owls—Juvenile literature. 2. Birds—North America—Juvenile literature. [1. Owls] I. Title. II. Series.

QL696.S8S23   598′.97′097   80-27541
ISBN 0-8225-0293-3

Manufactured in the United States of America

International Standard Book Number: 0-8225-0293-3
Library of Congress Catalog Card Number: 80-27541

1 2 3 4 5 6 7 8 9 10 86 85 84 83 82 81

CONTENTS

The short-eared owl is one of the 18 kinds of owls that live in North America.

INTRODUCTION

There are about 9,000 different kinds of birds in the world. There are familiar songbirds like robins and orioles; water birds like ducks and herons; colorful tropical birds like parrots and macaws; and even birds that cannot fly, like penguins and ostriches. And there are about 130 different kinds of owls.

Owls look very different from other birds. They sit in an upright position and are rounder in shape than most birds. The biggest difference is the position of their eyes. The eyes of most birds are on the sides of their heads, but owls, like humans, have eyes that face forward. Perhaps this is one reason that owls have always been so popular with people—they look a little like human beings.

Owls live in nearly every part of the world except the continent of Antarctica and a few islands. People have been studying them for thousands of years, but there are many questions that have not been completely answered. Do all owls have a sense of smell? How do owls recognize each other? Are young owls taught to hunt by their parents? How long do owls live? There is still much to learn about these fascinating birds.

People are not even sure exactly how many different kinds of owls there are. Scientists do not agree on the number of owl groups or which group certain owls belong to. You can understand why if you think of the problem in this way:

Suppose there are 35 children in a room, and you want to divide them into smaller groups. You decide to divide them on the basis of appearance: all the children in each group should look as much alike as possible. How would you go about making the groups? You could start by looking at the color of each child's hair and eyes. You could study the shape of faces and ears. You could see which children had freckles on their noses or on their knees. As you can imagine, it wouldn't be easy to decide which group a child belonged to. One child might look so different from all the others that he or she would be the only one in a group. You would probably have trouble even deciding how many groups there should be.

Scientists have similar problems when they try to decide how many kinds of owls there are and which group a particular owl belongs to. They look at the shape of the owl's skull and its face. They notice the markings on the feathers, the length of the toes, the size of the ear openings, and so on. Then they give each owl a scientific name that shows which group they think it belongs to. This name

The barred owl (left) and the great gray owl (right) have been placed in the same genus because they have many characteristics in common.

is always made up of two words, usually taken from Greek or Latin. For example, the scientific name of the North American screech owl is *Otus asio.*

The first part of an owl's name tells what **genus** (GEE-nus) it belongs to. Owls that are closely related are members of the same genus. Great gray owls, spotted owls, and barred owls all belong to the genus *Strix* because they are quite similar to one another. Snowy owls are so different from all other owls that they are the only members of the genus *Nyctea.*

The owls in the genus *Strix* are a lot alike, but there are some differences among them. Because of these differences, scientists divide the owls into even smaller groups, known as **species** (SPEE-sheez). The second part of an owl's scientific name tells what species it belongs to. The great gray owl is *Strix nebulosa,* the spotted owl is *Strix occidentalis,* and the barred owl is *Strix varia.*

Most people who study birds divide North American owls into 18 species. (Some believe that there are 2 different species of screech owls, which would make a total of 19.) This book is about the 18 different owls that make their homes in North America. The largest of them can spread its wings to equal the height of an average-sized person. The smallest is much smaller than a robin. Some North American owls live where it is hot and dry. Others live where it is cold most of the year. Some of these owls hunt and eat rats, mice, and other rodents. These animals are the owl's **prey.** Others live mostly on insects, and a few are very good at catching fish. Some North American owls are **diurnal** (die-ER-nuhl), which means that they hunt for their food during the day. A larger group is **nocturnal** (nahk-TUR-nuhl); these owls are usually active only at night. Other owls are **crepuscular** (krih-PUS-kyoo-luhr), which means that they hunt in the early morning and early evening, when it is neither very dark nor very light. All North American owls have excellent eyesight and hearing and are very good parents to their chicks. They have many other interesting habits and characteristics, which you will read about in the following pages.

BARN OWL (*Tyto alba*)

If a farmer is having problems with mice or rats, a barn owl can be a big help. One pair of owls can catch more of these rodents than a dozen cats can. Some people who were studying owls wanted to find out how many mice a baby barn owl could eat. They found an owl that was just one month old and gave it as many mice as it wanted. It swallowed 9 mice one right after another and ate 4 more only three hours later. In one year, a barn owl probably eats 2,000 rats and mice. It's no wonder that some farmers put special "owl holes" at the top of their barns so owls will make their homes there.

When hunting rats and mice, a barn owl depends more on its hearing than on its eyesight. Some scientists did an experiment to prove that barn owls can find small animals simply by listening. They put a barn owl in a special room that was completely dark and let some mice run across the floor. The owl caught each of the mice on the first try.

Barn owls often get into trouble because of their appetite for mice and rats. Three-quarters of barn owls living in the wild die before they are two years old from eating rodents that have been poisoned by people. Poison makes some rodents so sick and weak that it is easy for owls to catch them. Others are strong enough to survive and to avoid being caught. These rodents may produce young that are even stronger. Poison may not be able to kill them at all. If poison

Two barn owls on a fence

doesn't work and most of the owls have been killed, what will keep the rodents under control? This is something that people should think about when they use poison to get rid of mice and rats.

Barn owls live in many parts of the United States, but they are almost never found as far north as Canada. In spite of their name, these owls do not always make their homes in barns. They also like quiet towers, old windmills, and empty houses. The barn owl's heart-shaped face has earned it another name; some people call it the monkey-faced owl. Others call it the ghost owl because the front or underside of its body is a startling white. (*Alba*, the second part of its scientific name, means "white.") If a barn owl suddenly flew right over your head without a sound on a dark night, you might call it a white ghost too.

An Owl's Hearing

Owls hear very well because of the special kind of ears they have. Most owls' ears are long vertical openings in the sides of their heads. Each ear has a flap of skin behind and in front of it. The flaps can be moved one at a time or together. They can also be moved in the same direction or in opposite directions. In some species of owls, one ear is higher, larger, and a slightly different shape than the other ear. This difference in size and location makes it easier to tell from what direction a sound is coming. An owl can pinpoint the source of a sound by turning its head and moving its ear flaps until the sound is the same in both ears. When that happens, the owl is in direct line with the animal making the sound. It can then swoop down and catch a squeaking mouse for its dinner.

The circle of stiff feathers around an owl's face also seems to play a part in the bird's hearing. Most experts think that this circle, called a **facial disk**, helps funnel sound into the owl's ears. (You can funnel sound into your ear by cupping your hand around it.) Other experts agree that the facial disk probably improves the owl's hearing, but they are not sure how.

Another thing that helps owls to hear so well is the silence of their flight. If the movement of their wings made a lot of noise, they wouldn't be able to hear the faint sounds made by their prey. The front edges of an owl's wing feathers have a soft fringe that looks like the tiny teeth of a saw. Most people who study owls think it is this fringe that allows owls to fly so quietly. They believe that these soft feathers make less noise in cutting through the air than the stiff wing feathers of other birds do. A few experts disagree with this theory. They say that even if the fringe is cut off, the owl can still fly silently.

HAWK OWL (*Surnia ulula*)

Some owls live near people, on farms or even in cities, but not the hawk owl. It makes its home in lightly populated regions of northern North America and of northern Europe and Asia as well. Hawk owls live in open areas within the cold evergreen forests south of the Arctic region. They are very sleek-looking birds and can probably fly faster than any other owl. A hawk owl has a smaller head and longer tail than most owls its size. It hovers in the air much as a hawk does and makes sounds like one, too. Only when you see a hawk owl's facial disk are you sure that it is really an owl.

Hawk owls are diurnal hunters for at least part of the year. They live so far north that during the summer the hours of daylight are very long. During the long northern winter, however, the days are short and the hawk owl has to do most of its hunting in the dark. This owl usually does not hunt on the wing, as some owls do. Instead of flying silently along, looking and listening for prey, the hawk owl keeps watch from the highest branch of a fir or spruce tree. If an owl finds an especially attractive treetop, it may return to the same perch day after day and even year after year.

From its lookout, the hawk owl watches the ground closely for prey such as lemmings, chipmunks, or rabbits. When the owl sees the slightest movement, it swoops down and grabs the animal with its claws, or **talons**, almost always catching it on the first try. Like most owls, the hawk owl

From its perch in a tree, a hawk owl watches for prey.

usually kills by plunging its sharp talons deep into the body of its prey. When necessary, owls can also break an animal's neck with their strong beaks. Some hawk owls have another method of hunting. They have learned to keep an eye on people who come into their wilderness territory to hunt game birds. When the humans shoot down a bird, a hawk owl will snatch it up before the hunters can get to it.

An Owl's Food

Like all living creatures, owls need food to stay healthy, to keep warm, and to produce young. Owls are meat eaters, and they kill other animals for their food. These expert hunters take only what they need to live and to feed their chicks. After catching and killing an animal, an owl will usually take it to the branch of a nearby tree. Small prey is carried in the owl's beak and large prey in one or both talons. When it is ready to eat its dinner, the owl usually swallows the animal whole, after turning it around so that it goes down head first. If an animal is too big to be swallowed whole, an owl will quickly tear it into large chunks with its beak.

The fur, feathers, teeth, claws, and bones that owls swallow are of no use to them. Their stomachs cannot even digest such things. Luckily, owls have an unusual disposal system that works very well in getting rid of this material. An owl's

Rats and other kinds of rodents make up a large part of a barn owl's diet.

stomach digests what it can of an animal and then gathers the rest into a neat bundle, called a **pellet**. Hard bones and teeth are on the inside of the pellet, while fur and feathers are wrapped tightly around the outside. Several hours after eating, the owl **regurgitates** (ree-GUHR-juh-tates) the pellet. This means that the pellet is forced upward by the stomach until it shoots out of the owl's mouth.

16

In general, the larger the owl, the larger its pellets will be. What an owl eats makes some difference too. Owls that live mostly on insects, for example, have small pellets because nearly everything they eat can be digested. Some owls, like the hawk owl, regurgitate pellets quickly and easily. Others, such as the saw-whet owl, open and shut their beaks and shake their heads for 5 to 10 minutes before the pellets finally fly out of their mouths.

Owls usually regurgitate their pellets in the same place after every feeding. Fortunately for people who study birds, this means that owl pellets are fairly easy to collect. This is especially true if they have been dropped under a nest in a barn or at the bottom of a tree that stands out in the open. By collecting a large number of pellets and carefully taking them apart, experts have learned a great deal about what owls eat. When scientists look at the contents of a pellet, they can tell if a skull belonged to a squirrel or a snake, if teeth came from a mouse or a rabbit, and so on. Studying pellets has proved that owls are extremely helpful to human beings because of all the harmful insects and rodents that they eat.

LONG-EARED OWL (*Asio otus*)

This owl does have long ears, but you can't see them because they are hidden under the feathers on the sides of its head. The two bunches of feathers on top of the

A long-eared owl with its ear tufts raised

owl's head are not ears but **ear tufts**. They are called this because they look something like ears, but they have nothing to do with hearing. Some owls have large ear tufts, and others have small ones. A little more than half of all the known owls have no ear tufts at all.

An owl's ear tufts can be moved into different positions. When the long-eared owl is flying, it holds its ear tufts flat against its head. Perched on a branch, the owl keeps its ear tufts down until it is disturbed by something. At the first hint of danger, the ear tufts go straight up, perhaps as a way of telling other owls in the area that something is wrong. When a long-eared owl raises its ear tufts and stares straight ahead, it seems to look like an angry person. Maybe this is why people in Czechoslovakia say to their angry friends, "Don't look at me like a long-eared owl."

Long-eared owls live in a great many places in the United States, Canada, and Europe, but people hardly ever see them. The owls stay well hidden in the daytime and hunt for rodents and other small animals at night. Because the long-eared owl is a nighttime hunter, its hearing has to be very good. This owl's large ears are located in different positions on either side of its head. As we have seen, this is one of the things that help some owls to find their prey on the darkest of nights.

BURROWING OWL (*Speotyto cunicularia*)

If you are in a treeless area in the western half of North America and you see an owl standing on the ground, bobbing up and down and looking quickly in every direction, you can be sure that it's a burrowing owl. It's great fun to watch these birds and see how different they are from other owls. Even their legs are different. They are very long for the size of the owl and have so few feathers that they look almost bare. Burrowing owls are easier to find than most owls because they live in open country and are usually active in the daytime.

Burrowing owls often lay their eggs and raise their young under the ground. They use abandoned holes or burrows made by prairie dogs or ground squirrels. The nesting chamber is at the end of a twisting tunnel that can be as much as 20 feet (about 6 meters) long. Burrowing owls often lay eight or nine eggs, many more than most owls. Keeping the eggs warm until they hatch is usually the job of the female owls in most species, but male burrowing owls sit on the eggs as much as the females do.

When burrowing owls are not busy keeping their eggs warm or taking care of their chicks, they spend most of their time hunting. The owls grab insects in the air and also catch a very large number of rats, mice, and the small rodents called voles. Sometimes they eat the juicy fruit of the prickly pear cactus. Whenever food is plentiful, burrowing owls

Burrowing owls have longer legs than most other owls.

will even store an extra supply for later meals, an unusual habit for an owl. Some people who were studying these owls once opened a burrow and found that it contained more than 75 dead mice and other small animals. During the winter, as many as 20 burrowing owls may live together in one burrow, sharing the stored food when bad weather keeps them from hunting. This is another unusual habit of the burrowing owl, since most other owls spend the winter alone.

If you put your hand into a burrowing owl's tunnel, you are likely to jump back in fright when you hear a noise that sounds just like a rattlesnake. In fact, the sound is a warning call telling intruders to keep away from the owl's hole. Of all the owls, only the burrowing owl makes this unusual and terrifying sound. Chicks learn to make it when they are very young, and it works extremely well in keeping intruders away from the tunnel. Who wants to tangle with a rattle-snake? Owls certainly don't want them in their burrows because rattlesnakes eat both eggs and chicks. Even so, many people used to think that burrowing owls and rattlesnakes lived in the same tunnels because no one knew that owls could make sounds just like those of angry rattlers.

The burrowing owl of western North America has a close relative that lives in the prairies of central and southern Florida. It is smaller, lays fewer eggs, and is more likely to dig its own burrow. This owl makes a tunnel by scratching the earth with its feet and beak and then kicking the dirt backward out of the way.

The Sounds Owls Make

Most owls are very noisy birds. They hoot, whistle, wheeze, whimper, trill, moan, and mutter. Some even make noises that sound like puppies barking or kittens crying. Like human language, owl calls are a means of communication. Each species has its own set of calls, and each call seems to have a different meaning.

When owls are very young, they make chirping or hissing noises to let their parents know that they are hungry or cold. Sometimes they make snapping noises with their beaks. Young owls may also give a steady call that tells their parents that they are safe. If the chicks stop making this special sound, one of the parents will immediately fly to the nest. One or both of the adult owls may give a particular call when returning to the nest with food. Chicks can often hear this call before people can. Sometimes a male owl makes the same kind of sound during the time when the female is sitting on her eggs. This call lets her know that he is bringing food and is not an enemy.

Other owl calls are used to tell strangers to keep away. Like many animals, adult owls usually hunt within one specific area, or **territory**. Each owl stays within its own territory and will attack or scare away other owls that try to enter it. An owl lets its neighbors know where its territory is by giving a special call. Often other owls in the area will answer with their own territorial calls. It is as if each owl is putting up a sign that says, "Private—keep out."

Owls make many other kinds of sounds. Some are used to attract partners during the mating season. The meanings of other owl calls are unknown except to the owls themselves. But humans have been able to use owl language even if they don't really understand it. If you learn to make the special sounds of a certain species of owl, you can sometimes get one of those owls to come right to you. If you are lucky, the owl will sit on a branch above your head and answer every time you make one of its calls.

SAW-WHET OWL (*Aegolius acadicus*)

The saw-whet owl's common name comes from the sound of one of the bird's calls. Many people compare this call to the noise of a metal saw being sharpened. (The word *whet* means "to sharpen by rubbing or grinding.") This little owl also has a short whistling call that it repeats over and over, as many as 100 times in a single minute.

Saw-whet owls live in thick evergreen forests throughout large parts of the United States and southern Canada. They hunt mostly at night, catching birds and small mammals. These owls lay their eggs in old nests in tree holes. Saw-whet chicks look very different from their parents during the first few weeks after they leave the nest. The young owls are a deep chocolate color on their upper sides, while the

A saw-whet owl perched in an evergreen tree

adults are brown speckled with white. People used to think that the chicks were a separate species of owl. Now it is known that the dark-brown youngsters eventually grow up to be white-spotted adults, just like their parents.

People camping in the evergreen forests of North America often see saw-whet owls perched in trees very near their campfires. These little birds are so fearless and tame that they have been known to fly down and sit on campers' shoulders.

BOREAL OWL (*Aegolius funereus*)

This little owl has several different names. In North America, it is known either as the boreal owl or Richardson's owl. *Boreal* means "northern" and tells where the owl lives—in Alaska and the northern part of Canada. The name *Richardson* comes from Sir John Richardson, a Scottish naturalist who explored the Arctic regions of North America during the 1800s. In Europe, this species is known as Tengmalm's owl.

The boreal owl belongs to the same genus as the saw-whet owl and looks something like this close relative. Like its southern cousin, the boreal owl makes its home in evergreen forests and nests in tree hollows. During the cold Arctic winter, some boreal owls move south to find food, sometimes going as far as the northern United States. Such trips are very difficult for the owls. When they set out, they are already weak from lack of food. It is not easy for the birds to find prey in the unfamiliar countryside along the way. Many die before they reach a place where they can spend the winter. But a few do survive and become strong enough to return to their northern homes in the spring.

How Owls Defend Themselves

Like most animals, owls always have to be on the lookout for enemies that might attack them or their young. How does an owl protect itself and its family if it sees an enemy or senses danger?

For one thing, it can try not to be seen. Owls can usually conceal themselves from their enemies by sitting absolutely still in a tree or bush. The feathers of most owls are brown or gray, about the color of a tree trunk. The darker streaks on their feathers resemble the markings of bark. This **protective coloration** makes the birds very hard to see as long as they don't move. All owls have a great talent for sitting without making the slightest movement.

Some owls, like the screech owl and the long-eared owl, can even change their shapes so that they look almost exactly like branches of the tree they are sitting in. When one of these owls senses danger, it sits up as tall as it can, straightens its ear tufts, and pulls all its feathers up tight against its body. Suddenly, the round, fluffy bird is changed into something that looks like a thin stick! To make its large, round eyes less visible, the owl closes them to narrow slits. Even people who know owls very well cannot find them when they are camouflaged in this way.

But sometimes camouflage isn't enough. When necessary, long-eared owls, barn owls, great horned owls, and some other species will try to scare intruders away. The owls

This young great horned owl is trying to scare away an enemy by fanning out its wings and fluffing up its feathers.

do this by making themselves look as large and terrible as possible. They fan their wings out in huge circles over their heads. At the same time, they fluff up the rest of their feathers until they look twice as big as they really are. The owls also hiss angrily and snap their beaks. Human intruders can find all of this very frightening, especially in a dark barn or in the woods at night. Baby owls learn this trick of self-defense when they are quite young. They often manage to scare people away from their nests even when their parents are not there to help.

Some owls have another trick that they use to protect their young. If a person or an animal comes too near the nest, one of the parents will quickly fly down to the ground. Then it will pretend that it has a broken wing or that it has just caught a small animal that is trying hard to get away. When the intruder goes to have a look, the owl moves farther away. The intruder follows. Finally, when the owl thinks that the intruder is far enough away from the nest, it will suddenly fly back to its chicks.

If nothing else works, owls will attack their enemies. They use their wings like clubs to beat at an intruder's head. Their talons are sharper than any knife and their beaks are very strong. Angry owls can be very dangerous, especially if they are protecting their chicks. People have been badly hurt and even blinded by them.

FERRUGINOUS OWL
(*Glacidium brasilianum*)

The long-eared owl and the screech owl hide from their enemies by making themselves look like sticks. Other owls fool enemies by pretending that they are dead or that they have broken wings. Of all the North American owls, only ferruginous (feh-ROO-jih-nus) and pygmy owls have masks to frighten intruders away. These masks appear on the backs of the owls' heads. The markings on the feathers look like two fierce dark eyes with a white beak between them. Because of its mask, the ferruginous owl can look straight ahead and still scare away enemies that might try to creep up behind it.

The ferruginous owl and the pygmy owl belong to the same genus and look a lot alike. But the ferruginous owl flies more quietly than its close relative. It also hunts in the early morning and the evening rather than during the day. When this little owl flies at twilight, some people mistake it for a bat.

Ferruginous owls live in Arizona, New Mexico, and western Texas, near the Mexican border. These owls are also found in Mexico and Central America. There they are sometimes called four-eyed owls because of the dark spots on the backs of their heads.

PYGMY OWL (*Glaucidium gnoma*)

The pygmy owl is one of the smallest in North America, but it is very fierce. It will attack and kill animals that are much larger than itself. Pygmy owls live high in the mountains of southwestern Canada and the western United States. They are quite diurnal, often hunting in bright sunlight. The owls eat large numbers of insects, but they catch small birds, mammals, and reptiles as well. Unlike most other owls, they often remove the fur or feathers of their prey before swallowing it. Another difference between the pygmy owl and other owls is the noisiness of its flight. The wings of most owls move through the air silently, but a pygmy owl's wings make a kind of whirring sound.

One thing that pygmy owls have in common with other owls is being "mobbed" by flocks of smaller birds. Small birds seem to recognize owls as enemies by sight. When they see an owl sleeping in a tree, they will fly at it, making a terrible racket. Occasionally they will attack the owl with their beaks and claws. This kind of behavior is called **mobbing**. When an owl is mobbed, it usually sits very still until its small enemies go away. Sometimes it will fly off to find a quieter place to sleep.

The barred owl got its common name because of the
striped or barred markings on its feathers.

BARRED OWL (*Strix varia*)

The barred owl is famous for its many different calls. This large owl can make noises that sound like dogs barking or people laughing and screaming. Barred owls are sometimes called hoot owls because of one of their best-known calls, a series of hoots that can be heard for miles around. Some people think that this unusual call sounds as if the owl is saying, "I cook today, you cook tomorrow." Others who have heard the barred owl's hooting say it sounds more like, "Who cooks for you, who cooks for you all." Most people agree, however, that the owl seems to have its mind on food. In fact, the barred owl will eat just about any animal it can catch. What it catches depends on where the owl lives and what time of year it is.

Barred owls are found in southern Canada and throughout the eastern half of the United States. In the northern part of this region, the owls prey on squirrels, mice, rabbits, and other small mammals. Farther south, where barred owls often live in swampy woodlands, frogs and fish are favorite foods. These owls usually hunt at night, and they can find their prey by using only their keen hearing. Like other nocturnal owls, the barred owl also sees extremely well at night.

An Owl's Eyesight

Owls can see well at any time, but their vision is particularly good at night. In fact, owls can probably see as well by starlight as people can in bright sunlight. Why do these birds have such good eyesight?

When we say that an animal sees well, we really mean that its eyes are good at taking in light. An owl's eyes can take in a great deal of light because they are so large in proportion to the bird's size. A great horned owl has eyes the same size as an adult human being's eyes, even though the human weighs 50 times more than the owl. Light enters a creature's eyes through the pupils, the holes that look like dark circles in the colored part of the eyes. An owl can open its pupils very wide, until they almost seem to fill the whole eye. This allows as much light as possible to get in. (If you look closely at the pictures in this book, you will see how large many of the owls' pupils appear to be.)

The eyes of owls and many other creatures (including humans) have two kinds of cells that receive light. The cells called **cones** respond to strong light. They are used for daytime vision and for telling colors apart. The other cells, called **rods**, are sensitive to very dim light. There are so many rods in owls' eyes that experts think they can collect 100 times as much light as human eyes can. Of course, owls can't actually see in the dark, as some people think. No creature, not even an owl, can see when there

The large yellow eyes of a great horned owl

is no light at all. But owls can see extremely well even on the darkest night because there is almost always some light for the rods to take in.

Besides having very good night vision, owls have other special advantages when it comes to seeing. They have a larger degree of **binocular** (bin-OCK-u-luhr) **vision** than most other birds, and this makes it possible for them to judge distances accurately. Binocular vision means seeing two overlapping images, one from each eye. Many birds have very little overlapping vision because their eyes are so far back on the sides of their heads. But because an owl's eyes are in front of its head, its area of binocular vision is three times that of a bird like a pigeon. (Human beings, who also have forward-facing eyes, have about twice the binocular vision of owls.) With binocular vision, an owl can see depth in its surroundings and judge how far away things are. This is very important in hunting and killing prey.

An owl's eyes are remarkable, but there is one thing they cannot do. They cannot move around in their sockets the way the eyes of many other animals can. An owl has to turn its whole head if it wants to see something on its right or left side. To make up for this disadvantage, an owl can rotate its neck much farther in one direction than a human can. Without moving your shoulders, see how far you can turn your head to the right. Probably you will be looking over your right shoulder when you have to stop. An owl can turn its head that far and then keep going so that it is looking straight behind itself. By turning its head some more in the same direction, it can even look over its left shoulder! This is possible because owls have extra bones in their necks. They can turn their necks so quickly and so far that it hardly matters that they cannot move their eyes.

GREAT GRAY OWL (*Strix nebulosa*)

Measuring from the tip of the beak to the tip of the tail, the great gray owl is the largest of the 18 North American owls. Its average length is about 2½ feet (75 centimeters). But if you could pick up a great gray owl, you would probably be surprised that such a large bird can weigh so little. Its average weight is under 3 pounds (1,400 grams). The owl looks massive because it is covered with a great many soft feathers that are very fluffy. Sometimes they are as much as 2½ inches (between 6 and 7 centimeters) thick, thicker than a down parka.

Great gray owls live in the northern woods of Canada, and they need all of those thick feathers to keep the cold out when the temperature is far below zero. To stay alive in this cold climate, the great gray owl hunts and eats a variety of small rodents. The owl seems to find its prey by using both its sight and its hearing. Its large, perfectly round facial disk helps to make the great gray owl's hearing very sharp.

Great gray owls used to be quite common in the thick forests of Canada, but today they are hard to find. A scientist who wanted to study them had to spend two years and travel more than 9,000 miles (15,000 kilometers) through forests and woodlands before he finally found a family of great gray owls. Many owls of this species have been killed by trappers who believed that the owls were destroying large numbers of red squirrels. But studies have shown that great gray owls almost

The great gray owl is the largest owl in North America.

never catch red squirrels. A few of these owls have found a home in the mountains of Yosemite National Park in California. Perhaps the magnificent birds will be safe in this protected area.

SPOTTED OWL (*Strix occidentalis*)

Occidentalis, the second part of this owl's scientific name, means "western." Spotted owls live in dense forests in the western United States and southwestern Canada. These owls are usually smaller and darker than their eastern relatives the barred owls, but otherwise the two species look much the same. Their dark brown eyes set them apart from most American owls, whose eyes are yellow or orange. Both the spotted owl and the barred owl have yellow beaks. So do such species as the hawk owl, the boreal owl, and the pygmy owl. Other North American owls have beaks that are black, brown, tan, or greenish in color.

The spotted owl is not as common as its relative the barred owl, and not much is known about its way of life. It seems to do most of its hunting at night, spending the daylight hours roosting in tall trees or in crevices in steep canyon walls. Spotted owls lay their eggs and raise their chicks in these same out-of-the-way places, far from the eyes of human observers.

Finding a Mate

The mating season is a time in late winter or early spring when adult owls look for partners. Like many animals, owls behave in special ways at this time of the year. In many species, the male owl, or cock, has a special call that he uses to attract a mate. The hen, or female owl, answers his call, and sometimes the two owls sing a kind of duet with each other. These mating calls and songs are important because they make it possible for hens and cocks to find each other. A male owl cannot locate a female simply by sight. In almost all species, the two sexes look exactly alike, except that the female is a little larger.

After a male owl has attracted the attention of a female, he usually starts showing off for her. Some males bow in front of their partners or fly around in complicated patterns. These actions are called **courtship displays**. During courtship, the cock often brings the hen some food, as if to say, "This proves I am a good hunter and can take care of our chicks." Some people believe the male brings the female food so she will think about eating and not about attacking him and driving him away.

Following a period of courtship, the female owl allows the male to come near her. They mate, and the male owl's sperm fertilizes the eggs inside the female's body. After mating, the two owls begin to make preparations for the family they will have.

Experts think that some pairs of owls stay together all through the year and not just during the mating season. Other pairs separate during the winter and find one another again in the spring. In some species, owls seem to keep the same mates year after year until one partner dies.

Nests and Eggs

After two owls mate, their next job is to choose a place for the female to lay her eggs. Like other birds, owls raise their young in nests, but they almost never make nest of their own. Large owls such as the great gray owl frequently lay their eggs in old nests made by hawks and crows. Smaller owls are likely to use empty woodpecker holes. Some owls find a tree stump with a convenient hole in the top. Other species, like the snowy owl and the short-eared owl, lay their eggs right on the ground, in a hollow or on a raised spot.

Female owls lay different numbers of eggs and at different times of year. Some kinds of owls usually have 2 or 3 eggs, while others have 10, 12, or even more. In certain species, the number of eggs seems to be affected by the amount of food available during the mating season. In years when there is plenty to eat, the female owls lay large numbers of eggs. When there is a shortage of food, they lay very few eggs or even none at all. The time of year that owls lay their eggs depends largely on the climate in their area. Some produce eggs as early as December and others as late as July.

Owl eggs are white in color and rounder in shape than most other bird eggs. After a female owl has laid one egg, a day or two may pass before she lays another. Sometimes the second egg doesn't come until one or two weeks later. The female usually begins to incubate as soon as she has one egg in the nest. **Incubating** means sitting on an egg to keep it the right temperature until it hatches.

Most owl eggs hatch after being incubated for three to five weeks. The length of incubation probably depends on the weather and on the amount of time that the female is away from the nest each day. While the female owl is incubating, the male usually brings her food. In some species, the male incubates the eggs part of the time. Then the female can hunt for herself.

Before owl eggs can hatch, they are sometimes eaten by other animals or destroyed by storms. The eggs of owls that nest on the ground face extra dangers. They may be accidentally plowed under by a farmer or washed away by the tide when the nest is too near the sea. If their first set of eggs is destroyed, most owls lay a second set that same year.

Since the female begins incubating each egg as soon as it is laid, the eggs in one nest hatch at different times. The first one laid is the first to hatch. Sometimes the first chick is already three weeks old when the last one pecks its way out of the egg. Then the nest is full of little owls of all different sizes.

These baby barn owls hatched in the same nest at different times.

ELF OWL (*Micrathene whitneyi*)

Of the more than 130 species of owls in the world, the elf owl is one of the smallest. About 65 elf owls weigh the same as a single snowy owl, the heaviest of the North American owls. An adult elf owl weighs less than one ounce (28 grams) and is so light that it could perch on the end of a paper drinking straw without bending it.

Elf owls are very small, and their food is small as well. Their diet includes grasshoppers, crickets, caterpillars, moths, spiders, centipedes, and scorpions. An elf owl can hover like a helicopter in front of a flower filled with insects or catch bugs in midair with its talons. These little owls are definitely nocturnal, hunting almost entirely at night.

Elf owls are unusual not only because of their small size but also because of their traveling habits. They move around during the year, spending the summer and winter in two different places. This is called **migration**. Most North American owls stay in approximately the same area all through the year. They migrate only short distances or not at all. Some species migrate only in years when food is scarce in their home territory. But elf owls migrate every year. They spend the winter in Mexico and the spring and summer in the southwestern United States, mainly in Arizona and New Mexico. Experts think that the owls travel at night and rest during the day. It is not known whether they make the journey alone or in groups. The male owls get to the

An elf owl

spring nesting area first, usually in March, with the females arriving soon afterward.

Like so many other small owls, elf owls often lay their eggs in empty woodpecker holes. Sometimes an owl will look into what seems to be an unoccupied hole only to have a sleepy woodpecker scold at it noisily. Oak, pine, or sycamore trees are favorite nesting places for the small owls.

In desert areas, elf owls seem to prefer woodpecker holes that have been cut into the thick skins of giant saguaro (sah-WAR-oh) cactuses. The cactus plant helps to protect an owl's eggs from the extreme heat and cold of the desert. One large cactus may contain more than a ton of water in the fiber of its trunk and branches. In the heat of the daytime, the inside of the cactus warms up more slowly than the outside because the water keeps the coolness from the night before. The opposite happens at night. The inside of the cactus stays warm even when the outside air becomes very cool. The even temperature inside the cactus prevents an elf owl's three or four round white eggs from getting too hot or too cold.

Owl Chicks

When a baby owl breaks out of its shell, its eyes are closed, and it has hardly any feathers. Only two or three days after hatching, the chick is covered with very soft, short feathers called **down**. Owl chicks do not open their eyes until they are about a week old. Their pupils look cloudy or milky, and they stay that way until about the time that the young owls learn to fly. Then the pupils turn black.

After all their chicks have hatched, the parent owls are kept busy bringing them food. The adults tear large animals into pieces so that the little owls can swallow them. In a nest with several baby owls, there is a lot of competition for food. The older chicks, who are much bigger and stronger than the younger ones, often get more than their share. If there is not enough food for all, the older ones almost always grab what the parents bring before the younger ones can get to it. In years when food is very scarce, the bigger chicks sometimes kill and eat the smaller ones. In this way, at least some of the young owls have a chance of surviving. Otherwise they might all starve to death.

Young owls face other dangers beside lack of food. Frequently they end up serving as food for other animals. Chicks are in special danger if they fall or are accidentally pushed out of a nest in a tree before they have learned to fly. If they aren't killed by the fall, they may be eaten by a fox or a great horned owl. Without their mothers to

Like all young owls, these screech owl chicks are covered with soft, downy feathers.

keep them warm, they may die of the cold. Sometimes parents manage to feed and take care of a baby owl on the ground. A few chicks have been known to climb all the way up to their nests very slowly and with great difficulty. They cling to the tree bark with their sharp talons and sometimes hold on with their beaks as well. Young owls raised in nests on the ground can't fall out, but they can easily be caught by hungry animals. These chicks often leave their nests earlier than the chicks of other species.

Most young owls stay in their nests until they are four or five weeks old, but they almost always leave before they can fly. They stay in the area around the nest, exercising their wings and practicing hunting in nearby branches or on the ground. In order to fly, the young owls must lose their soft down and grow stiff flight feathers. This happens gradually, over a period of about six to nine weeks. By the time they have learned to fly, most owls look very much like their parents, only smaller and perhaps a slightly different color.

Adult owls continue to take care of their young for several weeks or months after they leave the nest. By the time autumn comes, the young birds have learned to hunt by themselves. Finally they fly away to find territories of their own, where they will raise their own families. No one understands how young owls know when it is time for them to leave their parents. A few families seem to spend the first winter together but nothing beyond that.

GREAT HORNED OWL (*Bubo virginianus*)

The great horned owl is so large and fierce that it is often called a "tiger with wings." Like its relatives the eagle owls of Europe and Asia, the great horned owl is a nocturnal hunter capable of catching very large prey. It can kill foxes, skunks, and turkeys, and swallow an animal one-third its

A family of great horned owls

own size. Great horned owls also eat rodents and sometimes wade into streams to catch turtles, fish, and frogs.

Great horned owls are found in almost every part of North and South America, except in the extreme north. There are about 10 small groups, or subspecies, of these owls in North America alone. The great horned owls that live in northern Canada have feathers that are almost white. The dusky great horned owl, which makes its home on the west coast of the United States, is dark brown. All great horned owls have the "horns"—really large ear tufts—that give the species its name.

Owls are considered such valuable birds that they are usually protected by special laws. In many areas of the United States, it is illegal to kill any owls *except* great horned owls. These owls are not protected because once in a while they catch chickens and other domesticated animals. Obviously some people do not understand that great horned owls, like other owls, do much more good than harm. For example, in the western United States, these owls eat the cottontail rabbits that destroy grain and other crops. There is another reason why great horned owls should be protected by law. People who shoot other kinds of owls often cannot be punished because they say they thought that they were killing a great horned owl.

Female snowy owls have more dark feathers than males of the species.

SNOWY OWL (*Nyctea scandiaca*)

The snowy owl is one of the two biggest North American owls. These huge birds have bright yellow eyes and magnificent white bodies. Male snowy owls can be pure white, or they may have a few black feathers. The females are mostly white, but they usually have many more black feathers than the males. The snowy owl's feathers extend down to cover its legs and feet, almost like a pair of furry boots. Most owls have some feathers on their legs, but snowy owls have especially thick ones. These heavy feathers help to keep the birds warm in the far northern country where they live.

The home of the snowy owl is the Arctic **tundra**, the flat, open area just south of the cold polar regions. Because there are no trees in this area, snowy owls lay their eggs on the ground. Their nests are often located on top of mounds of earth that have been pushed up by the frost. The chicks that hatch out in these nests are covered with snowy white down until they are about 10 days old. Then they grow a second coat of down, which is such a deep gray that the chicks look black.

By the time the chicks are seven weeks old, they have developed white flight feathers. These long, stiff feathers are mixed in with the gray down, which the young owls keep until they are one year old. But many snowy owl chicks do not live this long. Some are killed by cold summer rains. Others fall off the nest mound and die of exposure. Foxes eat some of the chicks. If food is very scarce, the younger chicks in the nest may be eaten by the older ones.

Adult snowy owls eat rats, squirrels, and Arctic hares, and they sometimes catch fish through holes in the ice. But their main source of food is the lemming, a small Arctic rodent. When lemmings are plentiful, snowy owls eat well and lay many more eggs than usual. In years when there is a serious shortage of lemmings, they may not lay any eggs at all. About every three to five years, there are so few lemmings that thousands of snowy owls leave the Arctic and migrate south for the winter. They often go to southern Canada. Some have even flown as far south as Texas and Louisiana.

Like all owls that are forced to migrate to find food, snowy owls face the dangers of starvation and exhaustion. Often the worst danger comes from people. Because northern owls like the snowy owl have not learned to fear human beings, it is easy for hunters to kill them. The owls are so tame that they may even allow themselves to be picked up by people who want them for pets. Unfortunately, owls kept as pets almost always die because very few people know how to take proper care of them. (In most places it is illegal to keep wild birds without a permit.) When spring comes, only a few of the migrating owls will still be alive and able to make the long journey back to their nesting areas.

SCREECH OWL (*Otus asio*)

Most people think that the common name of the screech owl is not very appropriate. This small owl has many different calls, but none of them really sounds much like a screech. In fact, its most familiar call is a long, wavering series of sounds that remind some people of a dove's cooing.

The voice of the screech owl can be heard in almost all parts of the United States. There are about 20 kinds of North American screech owls, including an eastern screech owl, a saguaro screech owl, and a Rocky Mountain screech owl. There are also screech owls named after the states they live in—California, Florida, Nebraska, and Texas. The owls are found in many different types of environments, from hot to cold and wet to dry.

Screech owls come in two completely different colors—gray and reddish brown. Pygmy, flammulated, whiskered, and ferruginous owls also have these two separate color "phases." This kind of difference among members of the same species is known as **dimorphism** (di-MOR-fiz'm). Studies have shown that two reddish brown owls can have chicks that are either gray or brown. Gray chicks and reddish brown chicks have been found in the same nest. But people who study owls think that the young of two gray parents are always gray. No one is quite sure why this kind of color difference has developed in certain species of owls. The gray and the reddish brown owls do seem to roost in places where

This screech owl has caught a vole for its dinner.

their particular colors blend in with their surroundings. For instance, gray screech owls often sit against the grayish bark of tree trunks, where they are difficult to see.

Screech owls of either color are also good at disguising themselves by changing their shapes. When the owls draw themselves up tall, their little ear tufts can easily be seen. The screech owl is the smallest of the "eared" owls in North America. Other small owls like the elf owl and the pygmy owl do not have ear tufts.

SHORT-EARED OWL (*Asio flammeus*)

Most owls spend their lives in and around trees, but the short-eared owl stays out in the open. It hunts during the day in fields and marshes, flying close to the ground on long, pointed wings. If the owl spots a mouse, rat, or vole, it drops out of the sky and seizes the rodent in its sharp talons. The prey is usually eaten on the ground rather than in the branches of a tree.

When mating season comes, the short-eared owl makes its nest on the ground, in a hollow surrounded by tall grass. Sometimes a pair of owls will lay their eggs in the same place for several years. They may bring a few dried grasses or reeds to line the nest. Like all owls raised in a nest on the ground, young short-eared owls are in particular danger until they learn to fly.

A short-eared owl in its nest on the ground

Short-eared owls can be found all over Canada and the United States, including the islands of Hawaii. These owls are closely related to the long-eared owl. As their names suggest, the biggest difference between the two species is the length of their ear tufts. The short-eared owl's tufts are so short that they can be very difficult to see.

FLAMMULATED OWL (*Otus flammeolus*)

Flammulated (FLAM-yeh-laid-ehd) owls are the only small North American owls with dark brown eyes. They look quite a bit like small screech owls, except that they have extremely tiny ear tufts and no feathers on their toes. In spring, flammulated owls lay their eggs and raise their young in southern British Columbia and the western United States. When autumn comes, they leave for their winter homes in Mexico and Guatemala. This owl's common name and the second part of its scientific name both refer to the "flame-like" markings on its feathers.

Molting

Like many other birds, adult owls lose their feathers and grow new ones once a year. This process is called **molting**. Owls usually begin to molt in late summer, when the nesting season is over. At that time the adults no longer need all their energy to take care of their chicks. Owls need a lot of energy when they are growing new feathers, just as young humans do when their bones are growing. The process of molting takes several weeks and is generally finished by the time winter begins. Owls continue to fly during this period because they lose only a few feathers at a time.

WHISKERED OWL (*Otus trichopsis*)

The whiskered owl doesn't really have whiskers. It got its name because of the brown-and-white feathers that grow out of its cheeks. These feathers have very bristly ends and do look a little like whiskers. The whiskered owl is very similar to the screech owl, although a little smaller. It used to be called the spotted screech owl, but experts have now decided that it is different enough to have a scientific name of its own.

Unless you go high up into the mountains of southeastern Arizona or southwestern New Mexico, you are not likely to see a whiskered owl in the wild. This species is found only in those two states and in Mexico and Central America. Because of the remote areas where they live, whiskered owls are among the few owls not much bothered by human beings.

The whiskered owl almost always roosts and nests in white oak trees. When one of these owls sleeps during the day leaning against a tree trunk, it is nearly invisible. Whiskered owls live near pine and fir forests but rarely go into them. If they did, they might be attacked by their enemy the great horned owl. This large owl often preys on small owls like the whiskered owl.

GLOSSARY

binocular vision—the ability to see two overlapping images, one from each eye. Owls have a larger degree of binocular vision than most other birds.

cones—cells in the eyes that respond to bright light

crepuscular—active at twilight or just before sunrise

courtship displays—actions performed by an animal in order to attract a mate

dimorphism—differences in appearance or size among members of the same species

diurnal—active during the day

down—the soft, fluffy feathers of baby birds

facial disk—the circle of stiff feathers around an owl's face

genus—a group in the system of scientific classification made up of animals (or plants) that have many characteristics in common. A genus is usually divided into several different species.

incubating—sitting on eggs to keep them warm so that they will hatch

migration—the act of moving from one region to another to find food or to spend a season in a different climate

mobbing—crowding around and attacking in large numbers. Owls are often mobbed by groups of smaller birds.

molting—losing an old set of feathers before a new set grows in

nocturnal—active during the night

pellet—a bundle or ball of waste material regurgitated from an owl's stomach

prey—animals hunted and eaten by other animals

protective coloration—colors or patterns on an animal's body that help the animal to blend in with its surroundings

regurgitate—to bring up from the stomach into the mouth

rods—cells in the eyes that respond to dim light

LENGTH OF NORTH AMERICAN OWLS

SPECIES	INCHES		CENTIMETERS	
	Maximum / *Minimum*		*Maximum* / *Minimum*	
Great Gray Owl	33.3	24.3	84.5	61.7
Snowy Owl	30.2	20.9	76.7	53.1
Great Horned Owl	25.3	18.4	64.2	46.8
Barred Owl	24.2	16.1	61.4	40.8
Spotted Owl	23.9	15.3	60.6	38.9
Barn Owl	21.1	14.2	53.5	36.1
Hawk Owl	17.6	14.3	44.7	36.4
Short-eared Owl	17.1	13.3	43.5	33.6
Long-eared Owl	16.1	13.0	40.8	32.9
Boreal Owl	12.2	8.3	30.9	21.0
Burrowing Owl	11.2	8.4	28.5	21.3
Screech Owl	10.4	7.0	26.4	17.6
Saw-whet Owl	8.6	7.1	21.7	17.9
Whiskered Owl	7.5	6.6	19.1	16.6
Pygmy Owl	7.5	6.3	19.1	16.0
Flammulated Owl	7.4	6.0	18.9	15.1
Ferruginous Owl	7.2	5.8	18.3	14.6
Elf Owl	6.6	5.3	16.7	13.6

Measured from tip of beak to tip of tail

species–the smallest group in the system of scientific classification. Members of the same species are very much alike, with only minor differences among them.

talons–the long, curved claws of owls and other birds of prey such as hawks and eagles

territory–a particular area in which an animal lives and hunts. An owl defends its territory against other owls that try to enter it.

tundra–a flat, treeless area south of the Arctic polar region

WEIGHT OF NORTH AMERICAN OWLS

SPECIES	OUNCES		GRAMS	
	Maximum / *Minimum*		*Maximum* / *Minimum*	
Snowy Owl	70.1	50.7	2,002.6	1,448.0
Great Horned Owl	65.7	48.4	1,876.0	1,383.8
Great Gray Owl	53.3	37.0	1,523.9	1,056.8
Barred Owl	22.8	11.6	651.2	330.0
Spotted Owl	20.7	10.9	591.1	312.1
Barn Owl	20.1	10.9	573.2	311.9
Short-eared Owl	15.0	9.2	429.4	261.3
Long-eared Owl	11.7	7.5	333.4	215.4
Hawk Owl	9.6	6.8	273.5	194.1
Boreal Owl	8.2	6.7	235.2	192.7
Burrowing Owl	7.8	6.3	222.7	180.5
Screech Owl	7.8	5.8	222.4	166.0
Whiskered Owl	6.5	5.1	186.7	145.6
Flammulated Owl	5.2	4.0	149.3	113.6
Saw-whet Owl	4.3	3.0	124.1	84.3
Ferruginous Owl	3.1	2.3	88.2	65.5
Pygmy Owl	1.8	1.2	50.7	34.6
Elf Owl	1.1	0.6	30.6	17.0

Adapted from *The Owls of North America* by Allan W. Eckert (Doubleday & Company, Inc., 1974)

INDEX